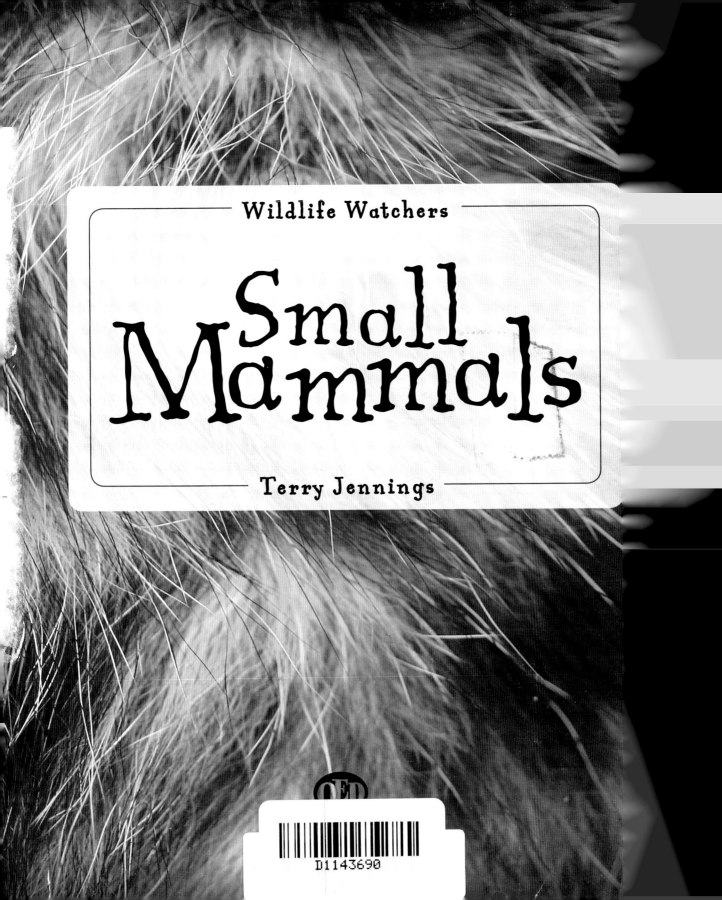

Wildlife Watchers

Small Mammals

Terry Jennings

First published in the UK in 2009 by
QED Publishing
A Quarto Group Company
226 City Road
London EC1V 2TT
www.qed-publishing.co.uk

ISBN 978 1 84835 236 0

Author Terry Jennings
Consultant Steve Parker
Project Editor Eve Marleau
Designer and Picture Researcher
        Liz Wiffen

Publisher Steve Evans
Creative Director Zeta Davies
Managing Editor Amanda Askew

Printed and bound in China

Picture credits
Key: t=top, b=bottom, r=right, l=left, c=centre

Alamy 5b wildlife GmbH, 5r Dave Bevan,
6t blickwinkel/Delpho, 9t D.Robert Franz, 14b
Arco Images/ Reinhard, H., 15c tbkmedia.
de, 23b McPHoto/WoodyStock, 23t Andrew
Darrington, 24r Renee Morris, 27r WildPictures,
29r Terry Fincher.Photo Int, 32b Arco Images/
Reinhard, H.

NHPA 21t Mark Bowler, 27b Alan Williams,
28t Michael Leach and Meriel Lland

Photolibrary 3r Mark Hamblin, 9c Brian
Kenney, 12c Juniors Bildarchiv,
22l Mark Hamblin

Shutterstock 2t gallimaufry, 4l Nik Niklz,
5c David Hilcher, 5l Ultrashock, 7b Emily
Veinglory, 8r Eric Isselée, 10l Dwight Smith,
11b ajt, 15t Ronnie Howard, 16c Herbert
Kratky, 18c Keith Naylor, 20c Oleg Kozlov &
Sophy Kozlova, 25c Tramper, 26l javarman,
26r gallimaufry, 28–29 Pixinstock,

StockXchange 12–13 tome213,
18–19 andres_ol

The words in **bold** are
explained in the glossary
on page 30.

Contents

What is a mammal? 4

Be a mammal watcher 6

The red fox 8

Cats 10

Water mammals 12

Weasels and stoats 14

Rabbits and hares 16

Squirrels 18

Brown rats and house mice 20

Mice and voles 22

Shrews and moles 24

Bats 26

Mammals in danger .. 28

Glossary 30

Index 31

Notes for parents
   and teachers 32

What is a mammal?

Mammals are the only animals with hair or fur. They feed their young on milk. Mammals live almost everywhere, from the hot tropics to the icy seas. The sort of place a particular mammal lives is called its **habitat**.

← A polar bear's thick, fleecy coat protects it from the icy cold winds in its Arctic home.

↓ Blue whales are the same length as 3.5 buses!

All shapes and sizes

Mammals come in many shapes and sizes, but they all have lungs and breathe air. They also have a skeleton with a backbone inside their body.

A fox has good hearing and a keen sense of smell.

↑ These young rabbits are sitting outside the entrance to their **burrow**.

Senses

Like all animals, mammals spend their time finding food, keeping warm or cool, avoiding danger, finding a mate and having babies. To help them do these things, mammals have well-developed senses for sight, hearing, smell, taste and touch.

Young mammals

Most mammals give birth to several babies at the same time. They are called a **litter**. Some mammals make a nest for their young. Some burrow underground and make a **den**.

Did you know?

Blue whales are the largest animals in the world. They can grow up to 30 metres long and weigh more than 160 tonnes.

Length = 3.5 buses

Be a mammal watcher

Many mammals are **nocturnal**, or only active at night. They are very nervous of people. To see them, you have to search for clues about where they live.

➡ These tracks in mud show that a fox has walked this way recently.

Sit quietly

Another good way to see mammals is just to sit quietly and wait. Choose a good spot where you think mammals may appear. You could look for their footprints in mud, soft ground or snow, or even for their droppings.

Know their habits

To watch a mammal, you have to know something about its habits – whether it is active by day or night, where it lives and what it eats. If you spot a mammal, walk slowly and stop frequently to check whether it has noticed you. Make sure you stay at a safe distance from the mammal.

Footprint focus

Some mammals are only active at night, which makes it difficult to spot them. Looking for footprints is a good alternative – you can even make plaster casts of them. Find out how on page 11.

37 mm wide

Keep a mammal diary

These are the main tools you will need to be a mammal watcher:

- Binoculars to see mammals from far away
- Pen
- Notebook to keep a mammal diary

➡ If you see a mammal you do not recognize, make a sketch in your notebook.

Date	Time and place	Mammal	Kind of weather	What was the mammal doing?	Was the mammal alone?
2nd March	9.10 a.m. field of corn	Hare	Cold and windy	Boxing and chasing	With another hare
3rd October	8.20 a.m. the park	Grey squirrel	Warm and sunny	Collecting acorns and burying them in the grass	Yes

WARNING!

Make sure you do not go out alone at night to watch mammals.

Did you know?

There are more than 5000 different **species** of mammal in the world, but mammals make up only 0.3 percent of all animal species. Most species of animal are insects.

⬅ Fresh droppings, such as these of a deer, show that the animal has passed this way.

The red fox

Foxes live in all sorts of places, from towns and cities to the countryside. Foxes have very good hearing and a strong sense of smell. Although they can see movement, they cannot see still objects very well.

Do I look a bit like a dog? Am I a red-brown colour? Do I have a bushy tail with a white tip?

Red-brown fur

60 mm wide

Spotting foxes

🐾 You can often tell where a fox has been because it leaves a musty smell, like stale food.

🐾 If you find a hole about 25 centimetres high and 20 centimetres across with bones and feathers near the entrance, it may be a fox's den.

🐾 A fox's footprints are about the size of an average dog's.

⬇ Fox cubs leave the den for the first time when they are about four weeks old.

Family life

Although you normally see a fox by itself, it lives in a family group. There is usually a dog fox (male), the vixen (female) and her cubs, or babies. They live in a den when they are breeding. This may be in a crack in a rock or under tree roots. Sometimes the vixen digs her own den, or she may live in an old burrow made by another animal. In cities, foxes may even make their den under a pile of rubbish.

⬅ Fox cubs are taught how to stalk their prey and survive in the world by their parents.

Red fox

Head and body length: 60–66 cm
Length of tail: 38 cm
Habitat: Woodland, parks, farmland, towns and cities
Activity: By day and night
Food: Small mammals, birds, insects, fruits, waste food from bins in cities
Young: 4–5 cubs in one litter each year

White tip

Did you know?

At night, you may hear foxes barking at each other, or calling for a mate.

Cats

Cats can be seen almost everywhere. Most of these cats are pets. However some cats live in the wild, too.

Am I mostly ginger or black and white? Do I have large eyes at the front of my head and a pointed tip to my tail?

30 mm wide

Large eye

Feral cat

Head and body length: About 50 cm
Length of tail: About 30 cm
Habitat: Countryside, in towns and cities
Activity: By day and night
Food: Small mammals and birds in the countryside. In towns and cities, waste food from rubbish bins
Young: About 3 kittens in each of 3–4 litters every year

Spotting feral cats

- A **feral** cat is a pet cat that now lives in the wild. It could have been an unwanted pet, or a pet that got lost.

- Feral cats sometimes live in **colonies**, or groups, with other cats.

Pet footprints

As well as making plaster casts of the footprints of wild animals, you could make a cast of the footprints of your cat. Fill a shallow tray with soil or sand and smooth the surface so that it is flat. Stand the tray outside and encourage your cat to stand in it. When you have a clear footprint, make a plaster cast.

Make a plaster cast of animal footprints

You will need:

- Some plaster of Paris powder
- Strips of thin card about 30 cm long and 5 cm wide
- Paperclips
- Container for mixing
- Small bottle of water
- Trowel
- Old spoon
- Paint and paintbrushes

1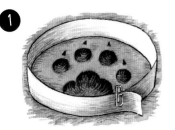

When you have found a clear footprint, circle it with the strip of card. Push the card a little way into the mud or sand and then hold the ends in place with a paperclip.

2

Put a small amount of water into the container and add the plaster of Paris powder, a little at a time, using a spoon. Keep stirring until the mixture is like thick cream.

3

Gently pour the liquid plaster inside the wall of card until it is about 5 cm deep. Tap the sides carefully to get rid of any air bubbles. Add some more plaster mixture if necessary.

4

Leave the plaster for 30–60 minutes to set. Carefully dig it up with a trowel and take it home. Clean and paint the footprint.

Water mammals

Mink live mainly by rivers and lakes. Otters live by lakes, rivers, streams and some coasts. Both mammals are nocturnal and good swimmers. They are **streamlined** so they can move quickly in water.

Am I dark in colour? Do I have a pointed nose?

Pointed nose

Chocolate-brown fur

25 mm wide

Mink

Head and body length: 40 cm
Length of tail: 12.5 cm
Habitat: Lakes and rivers
Activity: At night
Food: Fish, water birds, small mammals
Young: 5-6 young in one litter each year

Spotting mink

🐾 A lot of mink live in North America. Some were brought to Europe in the late 1920s to be kept for their fur. Many escaped and began to breed in the wild.

🐾 Mink eat fish, birds and small mammals, and will even raid fish farms for food.

Do I have a wide flat head? Am I brown with a white throat? Can you only see my head above the water when I am swimming?

Spotting otters

🐾 Otters have small ears, a long body and a powerful tail. Their short, strong legs have webbed feet.

🐾 Otters are very playful. They sometimes chase each other and pretend to fight.

🐾 Otters build their holts, or dens, near water. They are lined with reeds, grass and moss.

Thick, tapered tail

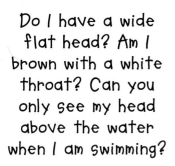

55 mm wide

Otter
Head and body length: 65–90 cm
Length of tail: 40 cm
Habitat: Near lakes, rivers, streams and marshes, some coasts
Activity: At night
Food: Mostly fish, but some frogs, toads and newts, birds, insects and small mammals
Young: 2–3 cubs in a litter each year

Webbed feet

13

Weasels and stoats

Both weasels and stoats will kill and eat animals larger than themselves. They have long, thin bodies on short legs. They can often be seen in the daytime.

Weasel
Head and body length: 20 cm
Length of tail: 5 cm
Habitat: Woodland, mountains, sand dunes and grassland
Activity: By day and night
Food: Mice and voles, rabbits, rats, birds and insects
Young: 5-6 young in each of 1-2 litters every year

Spotting weasels

- 🐾 Weasels are fierce hunters. They eat hundreds of mice in a year.

- 🐾 Each weasel's hunting area is about the size of 3.5 to seven football pitches.

- 🐾 Like stoats, weasels often stand on their back legs to look around.

- 🐾 In cold climates, weasels turn white in winter.

Do I have a long, thin body? Is my fur brown with a white underside? Is my tail short and brown?

12 mm wide

Short, brown tail

Brown throat patch

14

Did you know?

Even when a stoat turns fully white, it still has a black tip to its tail.

➡ White stoats are camouflaged against the snow in winter.

Do I have a long, slim body with a brown back and head? Is my underside white and does my tail have a black tip?

Creamy—white underside

Stoat

Head and body length: 25 cm
Length of tail: 7.5 cm
Habitat: Woods, mountains, sand dunes and grassland
Activity: By day and night
Food: Small mammals and large insects
Young: 6 or more babies in one litter every year

Spotting stoats

🐾 The stoat's hunting ground usually covers about the size of 18 football pitches.

🐾 Stoats can move very fast, reaching speeds of up to 32 kilometres an hour.

🐾 In colder parts of the world, stoats turn white in winter. They are then called ermine.

22 mm wide

Rabbits and hares

Rabbits and hares have long ears, long back legs and an extra pair of teeth in the front of their top jaw. They eat plants and rely on speed to outrun their enemies.

Do I run fast using my long back legs? Do my ears have black tips?

Black-tipped ear

30 mm wide

Large, staring eye

Spotting hares

- If a hare is frightened, it can run at a speed of about 56 kilometres an hour.

- Hares do not dig a burrow. Their young, called leverets, are born in open nests.

Brown hare

Head and body length: 44–76 cm
Length of tail: 7–11 cm
Habitat: Open countryside, farmland, woodland and mountain areas
Activity: At dusk and night
Food: Plants, fruit, bark and twigs
Young: 2–3 young in 3 litters every year

Look out for rabbit droppings. They are small, round and dry. Rabbits eat their own droppings to make sure they get all the goodness from their food.

Spotting rabbits

🐾 Rabbits live in groups in a system of burrows called a warren.

🐾 Rabbits can breed very quickly. In one year, a female rabbit can produce more than 20 young.

🐾 Rabbits rarely move more than about 140 metres from home. They eat away all the plants around their home, which gives a clear area to show up approaching enemies.

🐾 Rabbits have a good sense of smell and hearing.

Am I mainly grey or brown? Do I have a short tail that is white underneath?

Short tail

Orange back of neck

Rabbit

Head and body length: 48 cm
Length of tail: 5-7 cm
Habitat: Short grass or fields
Activity: At dawn, dusk and night
Food: A wide range of plants, including farm and garden crops
Young: Up to 7 young in each of 3-5 litters every year

22 mm wide

Squirrels

Squirrels are among the most common wild mammals in the town and countryside. They are easily recognized by their bushy tails.

Am I mainly grey or yellow-brown? Do I have a bushy tail?

22 mm wide

Sharp claws

Bushy tail

Spotting grey squirrels

🐾 The natural home of grey squirrels is eastern North America. Grey squirrels were introduced into Europe in the 19th century.

🐾 Grey squirrels have few natural enemies in Europe. They have spread almost everywhere, including parks and gardens.

Grey squirrel

Head and body length: 23–30 cm
Length of tail: 21–23 cm
Habitat: Trees, hedgerows, parks and gardens in towns and cities
Activity: By day
Food: Mainly nuts and seeds, also insects and birds' eggs
Young: Up to 7 young in each of 2 litters every year

Spotting red squirrels

🐾 Until the arrival of grey squirrels, the only squirrels in Europe were red squirrels.

🐾 Red squirrels are a red or chestnut colour with a tail that is much bushier than that of the grey squirrel.

🐾 Red squirrels are most likely to be seen in forests of pine, spruce or larch trees.

Am I a red or chestnut colour with a white underside? Is my bushy tail red-brown? Do I have ear tufts?

25 mm wide

Ear tufts

Watch it!

Look out for pine cones that have been chewed by squirrels. Usually only the centre of the cone is left. Hazelnuts eaten by squirrels are usually split into two halves. Grey squirrels often use a tree stump as a table.

Red squirrel

Head and body length: 20 cm
Length of tail: 18 cm
Habitat: Forests
Activity: By day
Food: Mainly conifer cones, fruits and nuts
Young: 1–7 babies in 2 litters every year

Chewed pine cone

Bushy tail

19

Brown rats and house mice

Do I have grey-brown fur and small, hairy ears? Is my tail thick and scaly?

Grey-brown fur

Thick, scaly tail

Mice and rats can be found almost anywhere in the world. The brown or common rat and house mouse are known as pests.

25 mm wide

Spotting brown rats

🐾 Rats often live on farms, on rubbish tips, or along muddy shores where food is washed up by the tides.

🐾 Many brown rats live in sewers. Here, they are likely to catch diseases, which they may spread.

🐾 A female rat can have up to 50 young each year.

Brown rat

Head and body length: Up to 28 cm
Length of tail: 23 cm
Habitat: Buildings, sewers, on rubbish tips and on farms
Activity: At night
Food: Almost anything, including stored human and animal food
Young: Up to 11 young in each of 5 litters every year

Greasy fur

Do I have large ears, a pointed nose and a long, scaly tail? Is my grey-brown fur greasy?

Pointed nose

10 mm wide

House mouse

Head and body length: About 8 cm
Length of tail: About 8 cm
Habitat: Buildings in winter, in hedgerows and on farmland in summer
Activity: At night
Food: Grass, plants, insects, human food
Young: 5-10 litters a year with 5-6 young in each litter

WARNING!

Do not touch wild rats and mice or anything that they may have touched.

Spotting house mice

- House mice have a strong, musty, or stale, smell and greasy fur.

- Mice are often found near food stores. They often spoil the food with their urine and droppings.

- In summer, house mice may live in fields and hedgerows. Most of them spend the winter in buildings.

Did you know?

Although brown rats only weigh about 700 grams, three of them can eat as much food as one adult human being.

Mice and voles

Wood, or deer, mice and voles live in wooded and grassy areas. They have many **predators** so the only way they can survive is by producing large numbers of young.

Spotting mice and voles

🐾 A wood mouse has large back feet, which allow it to leap like a tiny kangaroo.

🐾 Although it is small, a field vole is very aggressive. It makes loud squeaks and chattering noises to frighten other field voles away from its territory.

🐾 Each bank vole stays very near its nest. It usually goes no more than 50 metres from it.

Do I have grey-brown fur and a very short tail? Do I have a blunt nose?

Blunt nose

Long whiskers

10 mm wide

Field vole

Head and body length: About 10 cm
Length of tail: About 4 cm
Habitat: Mainly overgrown fields and rough grassland
Activity: By day and night
Food: Mainly grasses
Young: 4-6 young in each of 4-5 litters every year

Am I small with a sandy-brown coat? Are my eyes and ears large?

Large ear

Long tail

Did you know?

The teeth of **rodents** grow throughout their life. They do not get too long, because they are worn down by the tough plant foods that rodents eat.

Wood or deer mouse

Head and body length: 8–13 cm
Length of tail: 7–12 cm
Habitat: Woodland, sand dunes, parks and buildings
Activity: At night
Food: Mainly fruits, nuts, seeds, some snails and insects
Young: 5 young in each of 4 litters every year

12 mm wide

Do I have chestnut-red fur? Do I have small ears and a blunt nose?

Small ear

Chestnut-red fur

Bank vole

Head and body length: About 9 cm
Length of tail: About 6 cm
Habitat: Woodland, forest and hedgerows
Activity: By day and night
Food: Fruits, nuts, seeds, flowers and insects
Young: 4–5 young in each of 5 litters every year

8 mm wide

Shrews and moles

Most small mammals spend quite a lot of time searching for food. Shrews and moles are some of the most active small mammals because they need to eat a lot.

Do I have a long, pointed nose and tiny eyes? Do I have short legs and a thin tail?

Spotting shrews

- Most kinds of shrew need to eat their body weight in insects and worms each day.

- Shrews have poor eyesight, but their sense of smell is very good. This helps them to find their food.

- Shrews have special stink glands to defend themselves against larger animals. The smell stops animals such as cats and weasels from eating them.

Small, rounded ear

Long, pointed nose

Shrew
Head and body length: 4–8 cm
Length of tail: 3–5 cm
Habitat: Hedgerows, fields, woods and parks
Activity: By day and night
Food: Earthworms, beetles, spiders and other small animals
Young: Several litters each with 6–7 young every year

7 mm wide

Find an area of grassland where moles have been busy making **molehills**. Which is the biggest molehill you can find? How far apart are the molehills?

Do I have short, black fur? Do I have tiny eyes and large, clawed front feet? Have I made a heap of soil on the surface of the ground?

Silky, black fur

13 mm wide

Large claws

Spotting moles

🐾 Moles spend most of their lives underground. They live and feed in long tunnels not more than one metre below the surface.

🐾 Some kinds of mole cannot see at all. This doesn't matter because underground it is dark all the time.

🐾 Moles have powerful bodies and spade-like front paws, so they are very good at digging.

Mole

Head and body length: 7–18 cm
Length of tail: 3–4 cm
Habitat: In the soil under fields, farmland, gardens and woodland
Activity: By day and night
Food: Earthworms and insect grubs
Young: One litter of 3–4 young every year

25

Bats

Bats are the only mammals with wings. A bat's wings stretch from the tips of the bat's finger down to its feet and across its tail. Bats can live almost anywhere in the world.

> Am I large with a red-brown head and body? Do I have a large claw sticking out the front of my wings?

Large, pointed ear

Large eye

Spotting bats

🐾 Colonies of the common pipistrelle bat can be very large, with more than 1000 bats in a group.

🐾 In warm places, little brown bats do not **hibernate** in winter. In cold places, they **migrate** hundreds of kilometres in autumn to warmer places where they can hibernate.

🐾 The greater fruit bat has the largest wingspan of any bat.

🐾 Most bats feed on insects, but some, such as vampire bats in South and Central America, take blood from large birds or mammals.

Greater fruit bat

Head and body length: 35–40 cm
Wingspan: 150 cm
Habitat: Tropical forest and scrub in South and Southeast Asia
Activity: At night
Food: Fruit
Young: One every year

Am I very small and mainly orange or grey brown? Do I have short, broad ears and narrow wings?

Common pipistrelle bat

Head and body length: 3–4.5 cm
Wingspan: 19–25 cm
Habitat: Found in large colonies in house lofts, farm buildings, church roofs and other buildings in Europe and Asia
Activity: At night
Food: Flying insects
Young: One every year

Short, broad ear

Tiny eye

Long, pointed ear

Am I small and mainly dark brown with a light-coloured underside? Do I have large ears on the sides of my head?

Dark-brown back

Little brown bat

Head and body length: 4 cm
Wingspan: 14–18 cm
Habitat: Forests and built-up areas in North America
Activity: At night
Food: Flying insects
Young: 1–2 every year

Mammals in danger

About one-quarter of all species of mammal in the world are in danger of dying out altogether. This is called **extinction**. Most of these mammals are under threat, because of things that humans do. The three biggest threats to mammals are having their homes destroyed, being hunted or being harmed by litter and other wastes.

⬇ Red squirrels can live only where there are pine, fir or spruce trees, with beech or oak trees nearby to provide them with food.

Habitat loss

One reason why there are fewer red squirrels is the loss of habitats such as woodland. When large areas of forest are cleared, red squirrels may have nowhere to go.

← There are only a few hundred mountain gorillas left in the world. Most of the forests where they live have been destroyed.

Hunting

In some parts of the world, many mammals are killed for their meat, fur, horns or tusks, or just for fun. In some countries, mammals are killed so that parts of their bodies can be used as medicines.

→ This oil-soaked otter has been rescued. If its fur can be cleaned, it may survive.

Did you know?

At least a quarter of the 5400 different kinds of mammal are in danger of becoming extinct.

Watch it!

You can help wild mammals by not leaving litter that might damage their habitat or injure them. Mammals can get their heads trapped inside cans, drink cartons or plastic cups when looking for food.

Pollution

Many mammals have been harmed by chemicals used on farms to kill pests and weeds. At sea, **pollution** such as oil spills from ships kills whales, dolphins, porpoises and otters. Litter can be harmful to mammals and other wildlife. Broken bottles can cut mammals when they are looking for food.

Glossary

Burrow An underground shelter dug by an animal.

Colony A group of animals of the same species living together.

Den The home of a wild animal.

Extinction Not in existence any more. A species is extinct when no members of it are left alive.

Feral A pet or farm animal that now lives in the wild.

Habitat Where an animal or plant lives.

Hibernate To spend winter in a sleepy state.

Litter A group of mammal babies born at the same time.

Migrate To make a long journey, at certain times, in search of food, a warmer climate or somewhere to breed.

Molehill A heap of soil produced from time to time, as a mole digs its tunnel under the ground.

Nocturnal Mainly active at night.

Pollution Harmful substances that damage the environment.

Predator An animal that lives by hunting other animals.

Rodent A small animal that has a pair of incisor teeth on both the upper and lower jaw.

Species Any one kind of animal or plant.

Streamlined Shaped to move smoothly and quickly through air or water.

Index

bank vole 22, 23
bats 26–27
blue whale 4, 5
brown rat 20, 21

camouflage 15
cats 10–11, 24
colonies 10, 26, 30
common pipistrelle
        bat 26, 27
common rat 20

deer 7
deer mice 22, 23
dens 8, 9, 13
duck-billed platypus
        5

ermine 15
extinction 28, 30

feral cat 10
field vole 22
footprints 6, 8, 10
foxes 5, 6, 8–9
fur 4, 12, 25, 29

giant otter 13
greater fruit bat 26
grey squirrel 18, 19

habitat loss 28
hares 16
hibernation 26, 30
house mouse 20, 21

leverets 16
little brown bat 26,
        27

mice 20–21, 22–23
migration 26, 30
milk 4, 5, 12
moles 24–25
mountain gorillas 29

nests 16, 22
nocturnal mammals
        6, 12, 30

otters 12, 13, 29

polar bear 4
pollution 29, 30

rabbits 16, 17
rats 20–21
red fox 8–9
red squirrel 19, 28
rodents 23, 30

senses 5, 8, 17, 24
shrews 24
squirrels 18–19, 28
stink glands 24
stoat 14, 15

teeth 16, 23, 30

vampire bat 26
vixen 9
voles 22–23

warren 17
weasels 14, 24
whales 4, 5, 29
wood mice 22, 23

Notes for parents and teachers

In the world as a whole, there are about 5400 species of wild mammals. A reference book for the small mammals of your local area, illustrated by clear pictures, may be helpful.

A visit to a zoo, wildlife park, safari park or some other collection of living mammals, or to a natural history museum will help children to appreciate the great diversity of animal life in the world today.

A number of safety precautions are necessary when children study mammals. Under no circumstances should they handle living or dead wild mammals, since they often are host to disease organisms or parasites. They should always wash their hands thoroughly after handling food remains, or any other materials that wild mammals have come into contact with. It is particularly important that they wash their hands before touching food.

Children should always be accompanied by a responsible adult.

Always use plastic jars and other containers in preference to ones made of glass when collecting materials.

After plaster of Paris casts of footprints have been made and dried (page 11), they can be cleaned with a small soft brush and then painted, using one colour for the actual print and another for the background.

Many mammals are active only at night. It is possible to watch such nocturnal animals with the help of a torch fitted with a red filter made of transparent red plastic or cellophane, or by coating the bulb of the torch with red ink or layers of the dye from a red felt-tip pen. Humans can see reasonably well in red light but nocturnal animals cannot, and are not aware that they are being illuminated.

Some useful websites for more information:
www.bbc.co.uk/nature/animals/mammals
www.sandiegozoo.org
www.kids.yahoo.com/animals/mammals
http://www.zsl.org/education/
www.nwf.org/wildlife

* Website information is correct at time of going to press. However, the publishers cannot accept liability for any information or links found on third-party websites.